REMEMBERING MY NAME

A POETIC JOURNEY OF BECOMING
2ND EDITION

JADE DANIELS

CONTENTS

CONTENTS

For the Ancestors, my mama, and
all of the Black femmes in my life

"Are you sure, sweetheart, that you want to be well?...
Just so's you're sure, sweetheart, and ready to be
healed, cause wholeness is no trifling matter. A lot of
weight when you're well."

TONI CADE BAMBARA, THE SALT EATERS

NOTES ON A PHONE

SOME ICE FOR MY JAMESON

What do I want?
I want that non stop flutter
That

BOOM BOOM BOOM

To go away

I want to say something
And not regret it

I want to write
Every day
And be good at it

I want to dance
And tour the world
And act
And sing
Rap
Fuck up a cypher

I want to strip
And go go
I want to love
And be loved

And not be so afraid

I want to be loud
And free

Fuck
I just want to be free

I want to play drums
And go to Africa
And shoot glass bottles
With small guns
And learn how to fight

I want to stop smoking cigarettes
And I want to smoke a carton in a day

I want to ride horses
And deep sea dive
In the Great Coral Reef
Before it is gone

I want validation
But I no longer want to seek it

I want Black people to win
I want a whole world
Just for Black people
To start again
What then?

I want to kill the patriarchy
I want to kill white feminism
I want to kill myself

I never want to die

I want to know more
I want to stop acting like a know it all

I want everything and nothing

I want to see black children
Run
And
Play
And
LIVE

Without knowing death
Without knowing fear
Without being traumatized daily
I want to have a Black child
I want to not be terrified for that Black child

I want to get married
I want to adopt

I never want to get fucking married

I want to date a beautiful woman
Who opens my mind and heart
And shows me what true
Love and beauty is
I want to date a beautiful man
And I want to leave him first

I want to date myself
And be my most favorite thing

I want to see my soul
I wonder if I have one
I want all the answers
I want to know the questions to ask

I want my neck to stop hurting

I wonder if they miss me
I want to get to the end already
Just to see what happens
I want to start from
The very fucking top

I want to stop seeing myself
As so important

I want to love myself
I want to **LOVE** myself
I want to **LOVE** myself

I want to paint
And take photos
And be featured in a museum
I want to teach
And be famous
Just to make sure I'd hate it

I want to be hidden away from
Everyone
And I don't want
Any one else
To know my name

I want to NEVER be alone

I want to live in a cave
Or on a hundred acres of land
By myself
Off the grid
With my dog Jak and a bunch of animals

I want to stop feeling like a fake
I want to know which move to make
I want to not feel so very fucking lonely

I want to rid myself
Of the feeling no one
Actually loves me

I want to be strong
I want to feel strength
In the moment
I want to remember
My moments

I never want to see my mother die
I never want her to see me die
I don't want it

I want it all
I want to do performance art
And get tatted everywhere

I want to fly planes
And free the prisoners
And let them fuck shit up
In a trade
For their lives

I want to see all the government buildings burn down
And the Cold warming their bones from the flames

I want to see those in power
Feeling fear
Real fear, for perhaps the first time

I want to see what created me
And how
And I
want to know why
Im okay with not knowing Why...
I just want to feel god with every breath

I want to farm
And ride motorcycles
And fix cars
And sing in a sold out stadium
I want to write a movie
And a show
And direct it

I want to fly far above this planet
And just
Sit in the silence of space

And then
I want to be able to decide
If I wanna come back down

I want to meet Maya Angelou
And Assata Shakur
Nina Simone
Billie and Nat
Harriet and my great great grandmothers

I want to stop being so hard
I want to stop being so soft
I want to stop being so scared

I want to truly not give a damn
what people think of me

I want people to smile when they think of me

I want to know home
I want to feel connected
To a culture
That is not steeped and soaked in blood

I want every fucking thing
I want absolutely nothing

I want assurance
It wont always be like this
I want to see myself as others see me

I want to read minds
I want to read hearts
I want to read palms
Is that shit even real?

I want to go back to high school
And fuck that one girl up

I want to swim with dolphins
Maybe go live with them
Under the sea

I want to be able to read in the car
Without getting so sick

I want to know
When I die
I want to know

How

I want to stop pretending
I want to know these things

But I can't stand the guessing

I want to be smarter
And more of a hard worker
And to not get so jealous
And a little bit thicker
I want a phat ass

8

And giant blue hair
I want a fade
With big earrings
And a gold front
I want flowers in my hair
At all times
And to not be so afraid of snakes
I want to get a masters
And a doctorate

I want to lay in my bed
Until I sink into it

Never to be seen again

I want to decolonize myself
F U L L Y

And not have to do it over and over
Every single second of every day

I want to make my own decisions
And stand by them

I never want to be wrong
I never want to know
When I am right

I really do want world peace
I want to see a revolution
And see them get
What's coming
But I want to be sure to know

That I am not

That we are not

R E A D Y

I WANT TO BE HONEST

I WANT TO BE KIND

I WANT TO BE
PROUD OF MYSELF
AND NOT FEEL SO GUILTY

And all I want Is a cigarette.
And some ice
For my Jameson.

I guess,
That will have to do-
for now.

Jade. Hotel Room. Oakland. 2017.

BLACK GIRL;

Black Girl
Don't cry
Keep it light

Be strong
Be brave
Be Nice

Be beautiful
Have confidence
Fight hard
Be pure
Super sexy

Not too loud
Just right

Don't fight
Don't cuss

Be yourself
but don't fuss
too much

Lose weight
Be thick
Be smart
Work hard
Clean up
Cook good
Have style
Have grace

Have a good face
Have some good hair
Give some good head

Hold it down
Drink it up
Smoke a little
Go wild

Don't cry
Don't cry
Don't cry

Love hard
Be there
Care for them
Make 'em happy

Dance for 'em
And Make it snappy

Black girl
Braid it up
Flow it down
Curl it tight
Get it right

Don't sleep
Get yours

Make sure
you smile

Make peace
Be chill
Shut it down
Hard mouth
Soft lines
Clean nails
Soft skin

Love whatever situation
you may find yourself in

Hold it up
Breathe deep
Work it out

Blow up

Black girl
All you gotta do is try

Always try

And never doubt
Or get stressed out
Or want to die

Black Girl
Don't listen to their lies

Take your time

Take your time

Take your time

DANGEROUS SPACES

I've noticed how
In large and dangerous spaces
Melanated people
Yes, We Black people
Go off to be alone
In airports
And restaurants
Hospitals
And government buildings

Places of wait among strangers
Places of 'civil society'

We go to the far corners
To the far left or rights
Those empty chairs
We search to find

For A place of solace
Of peace of mind

I've noticed how our beauty and solitude
Still pierced the space
Like sharp knives

Priced above our collective income

With Our Afros and Locs and Fades and Braids
Headphones in
At Gate 38

While our flight departs
At Gate 40

How our eyes look up
Every now and again
To observe
And ensure
We are still
Safe

I notice us all
I do believe everyone does
And has
For so long

It's close to impossible
Not to notice all that

Impossible beauty
And sought after solitude
And godly splendor
For the yt masses
That troll along
In this existence
Looking... teeth gnashing

Our arms crossed
   Like 'don't say shit'
And our beautiful juicy lips ina
   'Yes, You can get cussed the fuck out'
Purse
And our long extended flat feet
Tapping
In anxiety
Like not today
Like just let me be

But I see
How we
Stay ready

In this world of enemies
Of this evil we can't fully see
But can feel it's energy
Surrounding us
In totality

And we look up
After writing or reading
For too long
On our phones
Maybe sleeping
only to see

That they now surround us

Like wolves
With empty seats abound
Teeth gnashing

The Males snorting and sneering
The females coy and dashing
With knives at their sides

I see us
Yes Us
Black people
Who just want our peace
And solitude
In these large groups

In these dangerous spaces

16

Wearing our
Many faces

But wait,

We are jolted to attention

Our names have been called
Over the intercom system
With Our Afros and Locs and Fades and Braids
For a random search
By the TSA...

As the wolves drool
As the sharp blades glisten

WOKE UP FROM A DREAM

Woke up from a dream.
Something that must have been on my heart and mind
Since I've left behind
I've left behind.

Those people, places, and things,
Those ideologies

I woke up a year ago
Outside of Los Angeles City Hall

To the sound of a drum beating.

I woke up a year ago washing the dishes
Of a white man
Who said if I didn't stop protesting
He'd shoot me himself

I woke up a year ago,
In the hottest point of summer

When I swore I set the water
To a boil with my hands

When I broke the AC
With a rage
I was only beginning to understand

(as so much blood kept spilling)

I woke up a year ago when I almost
Drove my car off the Pacific Coast Highway

Cause I thought the water
Would wash my sight away

Cause I could've sworn I saw freedom
At the bottom of that ocean

I woke up and I gathered all my things

My tears, my rage, my power, my majik
I packed them up inside me.
Only to share with those deserving

I woke up a year ago
Surrounded by Black faces
When mine had been the only
For so long.

I woke up and I learned to love myself again
Perhaps truly, for the first time.

I woke up and to either side of me

I found
Validation and Comfort.
Love and Protection.

I saw

Blackness and Blackness and Blackness
Everywhere.

I see myself everywhere, now.

The dream I was sent last night took me on a journey:
I encountered all of my old friends

All pearls and satin
All silence and stares
Their golden hair I was once so jealous of
Now so dull and thin
Their skin all pinks and reds

And my throat closed up
And I revisited those old feelings

That bug I thought I got rid of
That ripped up snarled up feeling
You get
Trying to read minds

An apology of my existence
Already beating for release
on the back of my lips

I could feel this projection of myself
Get smaller
(I swore I was 5'7")

Losing all my things
 I had packed up so tightly

But then

I turned to my right
And I turned to my left
And I turned all around

Blackness everywhere

My people
My Kin
My space
This they can not take

I saw Dashikis and Lemonade braids
And fros and bantu knots

I heard laughter and cuss words

Stomps and claps and snaps
Then I looked at them
Feeling taller than before

Remembering this ain't the same shit no mo
I ain't the same one

And I watched those old ghosts
Quickly disappear

And I laughed and I laughed and we laughed

Without fear

Until my eyes ran water
And my head felt clear
And fire slapped across the muscles of my gut.

All my people came to surround me
And they lifted me up

They took all the things
Spilled out in a heap
And they packed them back up
Perfectly, for me

I put my head down in shame

For letting those ghosts return again

"Hey man, don't you worry bout that!"
"They come and go and that's facts"

I woke up drenched in sweat
My ancestors surrounding my bed

A smile cut into my face.
I woke up a year ago
And I pack up my things
Every morning.

I take out what was forced into me
So long ago

I need to make room

I need the space to grow.

I keep waking up
And packing my things
Over and over and over again.
I stuff myself full.

I wake up smiling
These days.

JADE
7/2016

TRASH KIDS IN THE CONCRETE JUNGLE

And we found comfort there
Among the vines

And trees
In the Bush

We found ourselves
Reflected in the darkness of the city
In the abundance of this land

And we keep Running towards

the deep lush of the plants

Breaking through the
Crumbling concrete
The police sirens

The barbed wire and debris
Of this Concrete Jungle

Finding our many Treasures
through its trash

SMALL QUICK AND COOL

I loved you
I did
When I think about it now
I can see so clearly
That I loved you

I did

I walked blindly through my days

I've been told great love stories
Heard the songs torn from lover's lips
I've read the books
And I've cleaned up the messes

But ours was small
Quick and Cool

It was over as it began
Quick and
Cool

Now I ache for you
I walked blindly through my days

How I loved you
I do

I was waiting for my big story
But You came in
Ripping and Roaring

Small Quick and Cool

And when I think about it now
How I loved you
And still do

I can better understand
The singer's beautiful cries
The blood written on pages
The fire gone in eyes

So I playback the days
Of your light
And your laughter
Your warmth and your wit

Staying up too late
Of talking so much shit

I play it all back

And when it was over
I was happy to let you go
Just as we began

Quick
and Cool

AS YOU SLEEP

I watched you sleep
You looked so peaceful
Nothing on your mind

While my fists were clenched
And my eyes dry

My lips set in a tight line

Peaceful sleep evades me
I get no shut eye

Because it is thoughts of you
That keep me up at night

angry at you as you sleep... because you'll never love me

I AM PRICKLY AND SOFT

Notes of citrus drip
Gleam
And glisten
over

The glint

 of my thorns

Sharp and at the ready

I am
Both

Sweet and Sour

Both
Sharp and Smooth

Both
Finite and Endless

I am both Prickly and Soft

Savoring it all

NON-PROFIT BUBBLE

Sweat dripping
Stomach clenched
I never thought
It would *feel like this*

Eyes dilated
Mouth Dry
Head aching

I stay frustrated

Spendin'
hours and hours behind screens

Wires tied up in my
veins
heart
clenched up from caffeine

I break down now more frequently
Feeling like an obscenity

Like I can't say how I feel
Without some passive aggressive penalty

(It's Violent)

I take the pictures and write the captions
of the marches
The trainings
And direct actions

Playing Witness to the Struggle

While I am covered in plastic

Smothering In this
Non - Profit Bubble

I feel like a robot
And the passion is gone
I feel like I can't breath
I'm not sure I belong

I watch the others
Tired and broken

With these work loads
Steady choking

Facilitating through grief
Eviction notices and heart break

Always tryna give
more than what we take

So we set the agenda

we check in
Turn on our cameras
And hit send

Maybe it will all be worth it
In the end?

But How can we get free
While operating inside
Industry?

The blood of the enslaved
Still drying in the ink-

On the money we chase
And make
And spend again...

1
2
3
4
5... Million dollars in.
No thought of reparation...

How do we shut it down

Reboot
Reroot

How do we get control of things?

What are the contradictions that must
Stay
What are the contradictions that must
Be confronted
Killed
And buried
Composted and reused

To nourish some new **roots**

When does a small thing
Turn too big

When does a good thing
Turn bad

How do we turn back ?

My friends and family
Still strugglin'

Wondering where I'm at
And if Im still loving 'em

House is full of folks
And the rent is still due

The crises keep coming
And I gotta make it through

Would we all be in this together
Withstanding this inclement weather

If the funding stopped
And the paychecks ceased
When the walls come down
And we can't find nothing to eat?

How deep is this solidarity?

Does this movement move with me?
I keep rolling on up that hill
Tightly wrapped up in my guilt...
Participating in this violence
Feeling stranded on this

Non-Profit island

-       *From the NPIC Mix Tapes- , A piece for the Center for Story-Based Strategy Fellowship*

CRACKED CONCRETE

Cracked concrete
That slight smell of sweat
The faint sound of drums
And the tap tap tap
Of spirit

Drenched in contradictions
And steeped with constant creation

How did we get here?

So much pain here
So much conceded glory

As the lights fade and flicker
And the moon shifts and wanes

The land holds us together

Even in death
Even in disconnect
In disarray and distress

they call us back to source

Back to one another
Back to the beginning

I wrap my fingers tightly

Around this wound ball of joy

I've managed to find in the wreckage

And I hold so tight
That my hands bleed
And I squeeze it down
Until it disappears
inside itself

So I dig
And dig and dig
Until it is ours again

.... returning from Havana, airplane somewhere in the sky over somewhere In the place called United States

IN SEARCH OF...

I've been
In search of
community

In search of roots
Rooted
Easy flowing waters

Riptide pulls

Of love
And support

So long
I've been a traveler

A dandelion seed
Which moves
along the ripples of the wind
and makes a home
out of where it lands
— — — —
Water both
Flows easy
pulls and erodes

Water
Both cleanses and destroys

I made friends with the fire
a tangible form of nostalgia

I found family in glass bottles
searching to heat my soul

to warm my sorrow

when what I needed
was

Cool Water

The aid of sacred elements

In search of

fertile soil
To plant
nourish
strengthen

My roots
My roots

Our roots

Another descendant of the enslaved
Born in a land
both
foreign and familiar

Disconnected
Removed
Disrespected
Unapproved

What am I searching for
What do I need?

The soil calls to me
To bare down and ground
to close my eyes
to see

But the sediment is loose
Rocky and Eroded

It feels poisoned
And alien

What am I in search of
I am

In search of community
In search of home.
In search of a death
and most welcomed
return.

I want you to know me deeply
But I am very afraid

I have been manufactured

I have been shaped and framed

Sometimes unable to meet
my Own
Gaze

As the pressure
Of Spirit
Cracks
And explodes
Creating deep fissures
valleys of the in between spaces
both
the above and below

My ancestors fill me up with water
douse all that hot fire
and temper it with truth

with reminders of legacy
in my blood and bone

How do I reckon
With this great pain

With all of this unknown?
all I know is ...

I am reborn
Every night
And I die again
Every morning

Forever in search of,
Our Mother's Gardens

IN MY DREAMS

In my Dreams
I followed through and
met you
In Palestine

We walked the narrow winding streets of Gaza
Ate knafeh and drank mint tea while we

laughed
Between translations

We put the finger up in unison
At the zionist soldiers behind barricades

I photographed your beautiful face
And the beautiful places
You showed me

I pet the cats and played with the children
With their brilliantly gleaming faces
Alive
Full of life
Then

And now
it seems I waited too late
Like the rest of us
And I watched too long

And now I can only wonder

How many dreams were lost...

what else lies underneath the rubble?

Crushed in the dark
Waiting to be revealed

Witnessed
And
Remembered

In my Dreams
We followed through and
met you
In a *Free Palestine*

THE DESCENT

LIFE DON'T OWE YOU A THING

Oh how she thought she was
important

How she wanted to be good
kind
meaningful

And give this dreadful world
Something it wanted to keep

But the chains are heavy
And the realization tenfold

Oh life

How I wanted so much from you
But you don't owe me a thing

THE BIRD

There was a bird outside my window
She sang to me
sweet   *sounds of spring*

She danced for me in Santa Ana winds

She called to her children
                        Sang her love to them
 She never slept
                        Never gone for too long
She carried life in her wings
Secret joys between her feathers

She sang sweetly to me
A constant companion

And Now September is here
And the bird outside my window
Is no where to be found

Her song replaced with a beating on windowpane

The silent burning of tears
 The urgency of revelation

I listen closely
For her song to return

But I fear spring is forever gone
I fear my friend has moved on.

DISSOCIATED

I see you bruised and battered

Tissue deep
 // Marrow disturbed

I see you *dissociated*

What year is this?

How has time grappled with these inequities?

I see you tired

Oh so fucking exhausted
But you don't know shit

Not yet

I see you trying

But try all you may
We dying out here

We losing

What's that mean?
As I scan the horizon

What does that mean?

As I transcend this space

As I think of my mother's laughter

As I cry on this Boeing 738
35000 feet into the sky

What's losing got to do with it ?

I ask as I
greedily hoard and protect my little piece of
something
That I've been granted

While here
While here

What am I doing while here?

Too many questions
Covering up the process of solving
Of digging and aching and going forward
I try to be discreet

But the blood won't stop spilling

Where
Have
I
Been
In 2018?

Where did I go?

SEEMS LIKE

Seems like one day I just
Woke up with this deep sadness

And it felt stuck in my throat
And it laid out all in my gut
And I been beatin'

Shitting pissing crying

Screaming it out

Ever since

HEART OF BLACK PAIN

Had a bad day today
The day that aches and pulls
You down

Deep
To the

Heart of Black pain

Where sweat trickles incessantly and
The blood never seems to stop pouring

here where the helplessness
chokes and distracts

While the vultures prey from above

We got niggas locked up
In cages of the mind
Spirit
and body

And Our bodies
ache
And strain and bleed

All over these city streets

And I had the kind of day today
Where I couldn't look away
Where I couldn't wipe the sweat
Where I Couldn't find the wound

The puncture

The source of the bleed

And so it ran
Incessantly

And I let the tears
Echo the flow
Of the waters
which drip
And quench the thirst
Of such hungry beings

And their drool drips
And mixes with the blood

Of my people

My people

My people

Talking to walls
Grabbing at smoke
Punching the air
Trying to stay afloat
As waves engulf

How can we move forward
When I am chained to you

And you are stone?
-survivingthepatriarchy

WASTING TIME//
WAITING FOR YOU

I watch the smoke curl off my skin
As the fire flickers
As the gold Jesus and all of his
apostles

Watch me

as I fall apart

I know the hot water of my bath
Along with my body temperature
Are the logical reasons

For all the smoke
Dancing
off
my
skin

But for a moment I wonder

If I am truly burning alive...

A SERIOUS MONOTONY

The ground is cold
On my back as
I lay flat And look
Up
At the sky That takes
And gives
              With no remorse

There's blood in my mouth again
I roll it around my tongue
Before I
Spit it out
All over myself

The mirror is foggy again

I don't know
If it's the steam
Or my useless tears again

I haven't seen the girl
In the reflection clearly
For what seems like years again

The night is hard again
And there's a body beside me

But I'm lonely again

A Serious Monotony

THE HEALING IS DONE WHERE THE WOUND WAS MADE

I was told I was a terrible fucking person
And a fucking cunt
As I lay reading Kindred
ignoring my brother

Then later
I listened to heart beats over
I love you's,
I'm sorry

And the stirring of Rose Water

I soak my feet and hands in blood at night
Hoping to be cured of this sickness

In the morning
I come up short

Breathless and more clouded than ever
Dizzier than I thought I could ever stand

And I've been packed so tight in the corner
Somewhere deep inside my brain
For over a year now

For maybe forever

BLACK GUM MARKS

Black gum marks
Sticking to the ground
A sign of forever
        Small monuments of men

The smell of piss and blood
Fear and misery
Permeate these walls
        Soak the boxes we live in
So far gone

Which came first?
The evil or the greed?
The violence or the hate?
The Man or his god?

And what will remain?

FALLING ASLEEP AT THE WHEEL

Undressing these layers
Slowly

Falling asleep at the wheel
I'm always close to crashing

I slap the back of my neck
To help bring me back
To help keep me up

My stomach rolls
With sickness

And the sweet stale smell
Of death

I'm always so close
To falling asleep

At this wheel
I do all I can

To stay awake

WHO I'LL ALWAYS BE

Dissolved in the ether
Waking up
Choking on my anxiety
I'm lonely
And I'm scared shitless
And I wonder
Is this who

I'll always be

BIRTHDAY REFLECTIONS

In my 24th year

I am finding out what loneliness looks like

The hold yourself tight

That talk aloud to yourself

To have someone to speak to

Type of loneliness

In my 24th year I spent my time

Getting to know fear

Not childlike fear

But true fear

The type that lays at the edge of your bed every night
Staring straight at you.

The type that sits with you at dinner tables
Eating off your plate.

I am finding out what it means

To know and to love yourself

And understand

I may never really get there...

Because I am changing faster than I can keep up

And I keep losing the

Places
Moments
And people
That meant something to me

And they slip out of my cracked fingers
Along with all that time

In my 24th year
I am finding out
What life might look like

Uncertainty and laughter
Late nights later mornings
Confusion anxiety joy and love
Oh that love that love that love

In my 24th year
I began to question if I would be able
To step up to life's demands
If I am able to
put in the work…

I hope to reach a concrete answer
Before my 25th

DOGS AND CATS

The cat's crying
The dog's crying
The humans can't stop crying

Some days All dried out like sponges
Most days a sopping wet sad mess

I've cleaned everything out
It's been bleached clean to the bone

I've sorted everything out
I've sorted everything out

I've tried to throw out all the nonsense
But it all comes back to me
In a swarm of black

I shout at the stars
they don't reply back

My throat's dry and aching
I can no longer scream so loud
The tears don't come in torrents anymore
Mostly one or two
Warm and quick and stinging

I'm all dried out
Used up and flat

My ears don't work
They're overcrowded with noise

So I sit with the dog
And I lay with the cat

We're all doing the same thing

Crying
Just hoping to pass the time

SAD IN THE MORNING

I awake in early hours
Searching for a feeling
That I fear is forever gone from me
I cling to my optimism
And hope for better days
But all I see is black

I want to strangle this snake
Inside of me
And charm it back
Into its blissful ignorance

But my skin is on fire
And my mind
Seeps out of my ears

I clench the back of my hands
Until they bleed
I rub my eyes
Until they water

I sleep more for some solace
And to get some peace and quiet

I just want to climb into myself
Never to be seen again

CLAWING AT STONE

My knees are bloodied
Sore and aching
From crawling around this earth
My fingernails long gone
Cracked and shattered
From clawing at stone

My eyes no longer run water
But are dry and clear
My heart has become
A trained dog
Who sits and stays at my will

The dust won't clear
The sun won't let up

My throat full of sand
My thirst unrelenting
My hands no longer soft and looking
But hard and clenched
Longing to hold
Anything

For the sanity of release

I find solace in glass bottles
a comfort in impending death

It seems I've become this mean world that surrounds me

It didn't take long

CRUSHING EXISTENTIALISM

I am being crushed by my existence
It suffocates me in the night

It surrounds me in the morning

consumes all my days

Something I did not choose

Hoping for age to take the weight
For wisdom or
for love to bear the burden
To have someone or something
To lighten the load

To dry the useless tears
To silence the anxiety

To stop time

My existence is crushing me
My bones are broken
My insides shards of glass
And my mouth full of sand
What is this?
What is this sick sad torture
That is life?
I can not hide from its immensities

A poet once asked, " What are we but killers and sufferers?"

Well what are we but
Stars full of dread?

What are we but hopeless and sick?
Stuck in our daydreams
And Swimming in blood

How can I turn myself inward
And not demand so much
From my cruel master
What can I do?

This is existence is crushing....

PETULANCE IN LOVE

The sky the color
Of the end of your cigarette
Swirling like smoke

Once there
Then gone

All ochre and black
All marrow and bone

Like the petulance in love
Like the anguish of joy
Like the terror in nostalgia

Uneven fingernails
Scratching at your skin
Wanting you to let me in

I wanted to swim in your blood
deep dive inside the joints and cartilage

I wanted to live safely in your skin
Wrapped and tucked neatly
Around the very fiber of you

I wanted that

Sweet milk of oleander
Sour taste of spit

I wanted to drink your poison
I wanted to be your death

RAGING WOMAN

I've become a raging woman
Clawing at my hair
And howling at the moon
Slitted eyes
Pacing back and forth

Sleepless nights

I've become an unforgiving **force**

Cut you off
Roll my eyes

I no longer am concerned
About your comfort
About your gaze

I am no longer concerned with you at all

I can only hear the sounds of my people crying
And I can only feel the pressure of necks cracking

Under shiny new boots
600 dollars

I can only smell hair burning
And the tearing out of edges
Skin rashes

And bloodshot eyes

I care only for those that walk with their heads down

For those who open their mouths
Only to have blood come out

I've torn down my idols
Set my sanctuaries ablaze

I am a night rider
I am a flame swallower
I am a raging raging woman

And I am coming for you

A BROKEN HOME

Crumbled foundations

                  A fallen steeple

Perverted holiness

Rotting In its destruction

Offering

        Revealings

Offering   Blood

And   Water

Offering Truths

Where is the truth here

Where can I find it?

When will have it?

A Black woman once told me

In this life

You born alone

And you gonna die alone

And so I drift in my loneliness

I Gather my broken things

Every

little

piece

I pack them on my back
I take them with me
On this path

In this distorted reality.

I can not make sense of
People
And their doings

Life
And her mercilessness

Everything will come together

In death
With Spirit

And so I walk
And

I release
I release
I release

U

You came in like a storm
The kind that both nurtures and
destroys
Cleansing and unrelenting
And I couldn't look away

I quickly
Dedicated myself to your all
I built shelter around you

An altar of
U

Enshrined at the center
Of my everything

I placed you amongst the stars
Worshipping your every move

And you showed me your calm center
Your easy waves
Your loving power
Your fearful might

And I was glad

I offered you all of my sacred things
I wanted to share them with you
To appease your rain

To give my self
The only way I've known how

I gave you my stories
My family
My home

I opened up my insides
And you consumed them happily
Blood and gold dripping from your lips

But it did not satisfy
It could not quench your thirst

Or calm your storm

I felt like your best secret
I was proud to be
Your hidden rope
An iron anchor

Perhaps I misjudged
My importance to you

your winds of change took
Me by surprise
They shook my foundations
And blew away my reservations

 I held on tight

tears in my eyes

I loved and was in love
Imperfect as it was

And I was glad

I knew you wanted more from me
As your winds hastened and chilled
As your waters poured and drowned
I knew you wanted me wholly
To consume my body

As sacrifice
As reverence
A final offering

And I knew I couldn't give it
I could not offer my body to you
I could not offer over my autonomy
And so you turned to ice
Your shards splintered and cut my body
Cut my spirit

this time you turned away

And left me bleeding
And alone

In your hands
My most sacred things

I missed that old familiar storm
So much
For a while

It was hard to notice
The light of my Sun
Shining
Radiating
Illuminating
Revealing
Healing

Burning away

And I cursed you
For the destruction
You left in your wake

And me alone
to sort
And clean
and repair

all the things your winds took from me
When you disappeared

One night
Another like the others
Drenched in my despair
Bathing in my own blood

I realized
U can not take
What never belonged

To U

I saw how
I found refuge in your
Storms

As I hid away from my own

And right there on my bed
I cracked wide open
And let it all pour out
Until I was dried up

Until I was both
empty and all full up
At the same time

And I still think of U often
I'm certain I'll never forget you

You haven't visited me
Not even the occasional shower
Nor A quick downpour

Not even a gust of U
on a hot LA day...

And I'm glad

LIKE FRANK

I asked you to Keep a
Space for me
As I let my body speak
The words
My mouth never could

As Frank held us
In our immensities
the air so thick
With things left unsaid

As my heart watched me
Watch you
Watch me

Dance for you
Extend myself
A last goodbye
Feeling it while
Refusing to cry

That night gave me hope
That we would figure it out
That we would choose
To do the hard things
Together

But you chose to erase me
You chose your narratives
Your hurt over mine

You didn't fight for us
You didn't compromise

And I am left
Still picking up the pieces

Still moving to Frank's sweet notes
Scratching up blood
On paper

Months have passed since then
and I haven't heard
A word

Those mighty walls
I always witnessed in great awe
Came down on me
Crushing and swiftly
End of Story

The ancestors took pity
On my hopeful ignorance

And sent me a dream
In which I was offered
the truth of that night
That you both lied

That you were already decided

And I was there
The fool
The emerging one
Dancing in their naivety

Struck Open
for all to see

And like the Fool
Thus began my journey

Of remembering
Of forgetting
Of shedding
Of forgiving

And like Frank

I went and wrote it down
I sung and danced it out

And I found relevance in the details

I found healing
With time

I'm not asking for any more space

From you

I don't expect a call
An apology
Accountability
Or your fullest **truth**
I expect nothing

And yet Sometimes
My mighty anger wells up
Out of no where
Choking the light out of me
Clenching both
my guts and my fists
Collectively

And then I breathe and
Breathe again

Thankful to know
It's always there
Simmering
Boiling down

the bullshit

Purifying
the toxins

Creating freedom through movement

You always rolled your eyes
When I played Frank
When I screamed along
With his pain

But I noticed when you'd
sing along with me
I noticed how you
played him still...
Because you knew
I loved him

Like the Ocean.
Like you.

Like before,
now,
And then

I knew you
I knew...

I always did.

Jade (07/23/2020)

AND THEN LIGHT...

LONG TIME COMING

Today I feel joy
And it's been a long time coming

Today I feel loved
And its been a long time coming

Today I feel purpose

I feel worth
I feel light

A welcome change from my heavy
misery
Today I feel possible

I feel strong
I feel power

Can not stop the tears that fall on
my cheeks
Can not stop the smile cracking my
face in half

For the first time
In a long time
I feel joy

And Its been such a long time
coming

THIS NEW MOON PRAYER

On this New Moon
I stand in her shadows
No light is found here
But here
there remains life

On this new moon

I wash the soot of this existence
away

It hides in the cracks And corners
It seeps and oozes
And slowly accumulates

Until its pressure
Weighs down on your chest

Until ribs crack
Until eyes bleed
Until you can not breath

On this New Moon,
I met death
But she had no qualms with me
She nodded
I nodded
And we both drifted off
In despair

On this New Moon,
I danced with the fires of Shango
We revived that dormant
Lying Spirit
Of a Warrior

We embraced quickly
Large drunken grins
Still split across our faces

From our meeting
From our reconciliation

I nod at them
They nod back
And we part-
Knowingly, only briefly
Smug and upright
Hungry and focused

On this new moon,
I can't find much light

But I howl and I howl
And howl anyway

We are all lone wolves
When we need to be

When the journey calls for it

On this New Moon,
I lit a white candle
I said my intentions
I sat w/ my grandmother.

 On this New Moon
I went to bed - unsure of what's to
come

But I slept soundly.

A roar saved for morning

THAT SLACK PULL

I touch my skin
Lovingly, for the first time

I brush my knots
Embrace myself

My new found obsession

I pull at the loose ropes
The slack tether of my ancestors
I gather them in my hand
And tighten knot by knot
My hands bloodied
My arms sore

Yet I feel lighter than ever before

The shame
O the shame
I peel the layers of shame off like
dead skin

I put in the work
To see myself as a person
And to love her
As is

OUR MOTHER'S STRENGTH

I got my strength from my mother
And like her

Time has shaped it
Warped and dismembered it

Time has shredded us
Altering us so

Our strength is no longer reflected
in our eyes
In our walk
And our demeanor

We have become frightened of
ourselves
Fearful of fate
And of loss

But like my mother
I go forward

And I think of all the mothers
Who once were
daughters

Our strength never left

It flows in our blood
Scarred in our skin
Tangled in our hair
Patterned in the curves of our
bodies

Our strength cannot be a part from
us
For we are its embodiment
One cannot exist without the other

So child,
Do not be fooled

They will tell you
You are not power

They will tell you
You are not beauty

They will tell you
You are not strength

But remember your mothers
And remember their strength

Go forward

And let nothing stop you

SCORPIO SOLAR ECLIPSE

My back been killing me lately
And it's kinda like how
My heart's been breaking me lately
And my neck's been unmovable lately

Can't get through the night
I just don't feel right

My minds racing
My feet pacing

Back and forth
Back and forth
On concrete

I can't look up

And my backs been killing me lately

Kinda feels like my spirit is getting too big
For this ole body

Like my skeleton
Making room
For

All this realized power
All this hard earned
Wisdom
All this back cracking joy

To fit

UNDERNEATH THE SHED

The excuses shed like dead foliage
Revealing us

Naked bark
Bare Body

To One another

How can we steward this Healing?
This Rebirth?
Something of a Connection

Still Sleeping,
Buried, *underneath the shed?*

PAIN

I cradled the pain
I birthed in the dark

Rocking back and forth
And holding tight

Reminding
Myself

I am not my pain

But this pain
Is certainly

Mine mine mine ...

SEARCH PARTY

I joined the Search Party
For myself
in the dead of night

Flashlights among the bush
Bloodhound noses

Silent desperation

There were pieces of me strewn about
From place to place

How could I ever recover?

I joined the search party
for myself
In the dead of night

Through tall grasses And Panicked glances
And now I drift like smoke
determined
Following the evidence

Never noticed I went missing
Never noticed
When I stopped existing

I joined the search party for myself

And no one even knows it

BROKEN BACK TOGETHER AGAIN

And just like that
It felt like I was all broken back together
again ...
I cried-
...oh how I cried

and felt those tears
clean out that gunk
had saved up in the corners

I laughed and
shook up them cobwebs
sprawling all over the deep stretch of my
heart and gut

I danced
And the light bursted inside and outside of
me so hot *it exploded*

Felt like I birthed **A few new worlds**

I watched as the gravity of me
Then swallowed those worlds whole

I stretched and
My shoulders made the land
quiver and ache

from being so clenched up all them years
From being so tense

So tight
So strained

My exhale blew over whole city buildings

And my stare
Erupted 'em right into flames

I held one foot in front of the other
And my head back on straight

And I sat there in this great power

All broken back together again

There's no shame in stopping
Nothing wrong in giving up
When your bones are breaking
And your eyes no longer clear
There's no fault in realizing when to stop
Take a break

And start again when you are able...

-stopping aint quitting all the time

I AM A MIRROR

 "I am a Mirror' She Said.
Looking into the glass portal.
And it cracked straight down the middle.

It did not startle her
Just the opposite

She drug her index and middle finger
Down the jagged cracks
Smearing blood
Obscuring vision

"I am Blood and Bone"
And as she spoke, her back cracked right in half
legs broke from underneath her
Gases and fluids popped and flowed
And released
Within her

A deep rushing forward
then through

"I am the Water"
And the sweet pure liquid poured from her eyes
Endlessly
It dripped from her ears and
ran like a river from

The 4 corners her mouth

"I am the Fire"
And her skin glowed
From the heat within
Until it cracked and sizzled
Her hair erupted into flames

" I am Nothing"
She chanted as she lay down into the Earth,
Disappearing into the ash

" I am Forever"

WHY THIS FIRE CHOSE ME?

I spent my days endlessly drowning
My insides dry cracked and aching

I hadn't felt or seen another in so long
Until I heard her song

I heard the fire call to me in the dead of night

A sound I'd never heard before
I had no choice but to follow and see
It had been so many
Months, days, weeks?

Since I heard something say my name
So sweetly

I followed in the dark
To search for
light
illuminating

When I reached it
It was just a small flame

But the room was warm
And damp

As I sat down before it
My dry mouth agape
My eyes unmoving

The flame reached up and out
Swallowing me whole

I screamed aloud

Thinking this is the end
Until I realized the flames
Were not burning skin

The very opposite in fact
The fire danced around my body
The flames licking every inch

The feeling I could not explain
It began to scratch that deep itch

I felt the heat in every Cell
in my body
We were now one
This room
My self
This light

I never even tried to fight

I opened my legs and arched my back
It felt so good
Thought I'd have a heart attack

But the flame whispered
relax
Let me hold you

Receive my light

As it burned I could feel
The dry cracked tinder inside me
ignite

And I laughed so hard
And moaned so loud
The whole house shook

The flame burned hotter
And warm wet water

Started dripping from me

Looking down at the crossroads
Of this mighty body

And the waters cooled and gleamed
Soaking into the earth under my feet

And in this moment
I felt alive
I felt free

Then the room went dark

And as I lay there breathless

In my ecstasy

I wondered

why this fire choose me?

DEVELOPMENT

I write the lists and the goals
I form the tasks
I set the schedules
I constantly think of how

Where
Why
How

I'm so behind
On my unending development

I bite my nails down to
The quick

My legs tap rhythmically
To my anxieties
Until they are sore

Then I pause
Because my coffee getting cold

And my dog
Throws his bone in my lap
And looks at me longingly

And my heart beats
So **unendlessly**
For now.

So I put the pen down
I pause the racing thoughts

I sip my coffee
And I play with my dog
—----

AT THE FEET OF MY ANCESTORS

I feel less lonely

Less achy

Less twitchy

Less ugly

Less wrong

Less inadequate

Less unheard

Less misunderstood

At the feet of my ancestors
And nestled tightly in the warmth of my core

SURROUNDING IT ALL

I don't want to be like the tree

In its intimacy and strength

I don't want to be like the water

In its restless grace

I want to be like the air...

Surrounding it all

TELLING STORIES AGAIN

I craft stories of my pain
And write fairytales of my fears
My shame.

I weave in and out of consciousness
I peak through my sprawled fingers

What is this dance with my
Fate?

Where has the light gone
From my lover's eyes?

Where can I find that
Comfort
That I once felt

Replaced by a dulling aching
An incessant **knocking at the door.**

Where do my tears go
Once they've all dried up

Crusted in memoriam onto my skin

My bed
My hands

I craft poems of my good luck
My fortitude and brilliance

I make legends of my battles
With Indecision

And oh ain't they epic

Im telling stories again

Because I crave for a love that
Will eat me all the way up

And I crave for an energy that
Can match my own

I want to lick 'round the edges of this world
Like an oyster shell

I want to roll around in the slop of it
I want to run away into the corners of it

I want to Let my life be ***the story of it***

REMEMBERING MY NAME

REMEMBERING MY NAME

Working on remembering my name
The one formed in ancestral fire

Working on filling up all these holes
Poke, prodded, and stomped in me

Working on sloughing off this dead skin, the
heavy vacancies, the rotting meat.

Working on. Calling on. Moving on.

Healing is my divine right and I claim it with
every breath.
I am healing timelines
and lifelines

I am healing heart and lungs.
I am healing. I am whole.

Cleansed in the sweet cool water
Transformed in burning death

I RAN TO THE FOREST IN SEARCH OF HEALING

I ran up to the mountains
Hoping all that hard bare
Ancientness

Could tell me
who I am
Who I was

I laid by the water
Hoping that beautiful

Rushing
Sacredness

Would wash me clean

Tumble me dry

And I'd return to my city home
   Renewed

I slept between the trees so that they may
heal me

Underneath Their canopy

I wanted to dissolve into the soft deep Earth
I wanted to sink down into that warm Core

I cried as time blurred
hoping my tears
or
The salt of my pain
would nourish those deep roots
And feel me...

Please please just heal me.

I danced by the fire
Hoping it would burn, crack,
 and clear
Away all the sickness inside

I needed it to work quickly
As I sipped my wine.

After so long
Sitting amongst those old gods

Still Sick and
Trapped
and
Caught up in my grief
 I looked at My natural teachers
        In disbelief...

What about **me**?
Where is my healing?

And they said
You might've came home
Look like you enjoyed that wine

But you forgot to do
That
 work

That Overtime

You go searching
For a remedy
One we can quickly provide

But are you sure you want to be well dear?
Are you ready to die and be reborn Alive?

Until you do the work
And stop with your lies

You must dig,
crawl,
push,
fight,
and love
You must
offer,
revere,
sacrifice,
and clear

F O C U S

and

R E L E A S E

Keep your eyes on your own paper
Stop tryna cheat

Healing like Living
Ain't no easy feat

Now lay down here and get some more sleep.
Before you go, just one mo' thing

You have all that you need for the healing you seek.

you must understand

What you run away to search for
Is right in your hands

What you run away to search for

Is right in your hands

ONE MOMENT AT A TIME

Take it
one moment at a time beloved,
if that's what you need

And never close your eyes on the day
Without noticing

The LOVE all around you

MAKING A FOOL OF THE GOD IN BOTH OF US

I won't prostrate
Naked and pleading
For your love

I won't speak in gnarled tongues
Cold silence

While my spirit withers

While your face remains unmoved

Trying to teach
a language your tongue can not seem to grasp
An understanding our hearts do not seem to share

I can smell your fear

And I know
There is a
lesson here

I trace the outlines of my grandmother's faces and their mothers too.

I swish the names of their mothers and their daughters in my mouth

Like whiskey
Like turpentine
Some root medicine
For my sick heart

And the taste is so bitter and familiar
So rich and outstanding
So full of the same
I can barely get it all in

What you frontin' for?

Why you so conflicted ?

Did my love not warm you?
Change you?
Make you want more?

And I felt you
widen and shrink
Shrink and widen

Your elbow locked
Setting arms distance between us.

Like child's play.
A roughhousing

I haddta remove you from the center of my world
Cause you set my gravity off
had me feeling so heavy

My Spirit Orbiting around
The questioning silence
The desperate glances

I refuse to lose the lesson in this
I refuse to collapse our love into one poem
One narrative
One beginning and one ending

Cause We contained multitudes

I will never regret the light I shone with you
The breath of life brought into a day to day

The threads I pulled and knotted
Tight
Like a fisherman

My auntie say
You got to know when to leave the party, Jade.
You got to get up when love is no longer being served.

So I quietly prepared
I washed myself in sacred waters

Until I could wipe my eyes and mouth
With white

Until I could get up off that ground.

Until I could raise my gaze from your feet
And excuse myself from this back and forth
of begging
Of bargaining
From this splitting of selves

And it hurt
and it tore
but

I don't regret it

Cause I learned how staying too long
when you ain't welcome
Where you ain't worshipped
Only

Makes a fool of the God in
Both of Us

SINCE I BEEN BORN

Since I Been Born
The world been telling me
What they think is best

I think it's best you just be quiet
I think it's best you just sit down

I think it's best you change yourself completely
And don't make a fucking sound

Go and Disappear until I need you
And you better not be late.

I think it's best you do ALL this work and labor -
and no you won't get paid

And we think it best you not complain or
need breaks
or rest
or a thanks
for your stress
I really think it's best

That you never yearn for freedom or seek autonomy-

douse out all that fire
that lives in ya chest

You should stay shackled here with me
You won't ever get the time you need
To figure it out for yourself
To flow and feel freely
Why?

Because that's what I
think is best.

I think it best
You just listen to me
And act accordingly

I think it's best you don't challenge my authority
I think it's best you just agree with me

I think it best you don't ask for accountability

Shut the fuck up and listen
While I tell you about
yourself
Your family
Your heart mind and intentions

I think it's best
That you dance for me
Care and entertain these niggas
Yea

And you know
I definitely think it best you
never say no
When I wanna fuck
When I wanna touch
or stare
or abuse

Or do some random shit
To prove my power over you

Internalize all my projections
Cause they ARE the gospel truth

Just be quiet and sit down somewhere

And Don't even think about
Asking for justice
 or support
 or retribution

And Don't speak to your dead

That's all an illusion

 No need to know your history
yeah definitely not that
There's just too much there
For you to ever unpack

I think it would be best
For you to just die

I should be the one to kill you
To make sure you don't survive

Yes, maybe that's best
But not until
I get what I need
And only after
You fuck me
Yes yes
O Trust me,
That That is what is best '
....
And I be like, nah.
(a poem about you weirdos)

Published in Los Angeles Literary Journal, Dryland Lit in 2020

STORM

I am not a victim of the storm- being dragged out to
drown at sea.
I am the storm-

I am the debris and the clearing away
And.

I am the calm on the horizon"

THE PROBLEM WITH ILY

The problem with I love you

Is the way the colonizer's languages
Ripped raped warped
and beat it away
from its Sacred beginnings

A romantic Destroying of Spirit

Ribbons wrapped up in it
bears chocolates
and bright red roses
Only $100
for 2 dozen

A three word dinner
We never wanted to eat
In search for it everywhere
 yet
Never looking beneath our feet

The problem with I love yous
Is how we wait on the words
But never see the actions

Or to see the actions
To never be held by the words

Separated from the masculine
Dismissed through the feminine

The Mother
As An embodiment

The Father
An antithesis

More White words
detached from
Their many meanings

Leaving destruction in their wake

The problem with I Love Yous
Is that they only hold weight

When the one with power
Decides
to gift it
To say it
Or to portray

Swung like a pendulum in front
Of our noses

Creating a deeply traumatic hypnosis

Oh how we wait patiently
for the words

to drop down to us from
The mouth of a lover

To flow down easy
Like the dripping of spit
On body

To encourage

More slip

The problem with I love yous is
That
We are terrified of the idea
of something being unconditional
In this extractive society

Didn't ya mama teach ya
Ain't nothing in this life come free

especially not u + me
With our offensively made
 Black bodies *
Giving and receiving Love
 abundantly

The problem with I love yous
Is how they can reveal what
We so desperately need

How foreign the idea to us
How difficult to see

That having conditions
Can simply mean having boundaries

Is a way to know
Who deserves access to
This sacred life force energy

Who gives and receives it
Who refuses and keeps it
Who deserves and reveals it

Who gets to define it

The problem with I love yous
Is too many children
Sit like dogs waiting

To hear it said to them
Shown to them

Sitting at their caretakers feet

Waiting To lap the words up
Like dogs in heat

Until that thirst
Is no longer felt
Until it is something
They no longer seek

Time makes liars out of us all

We only tell ourselves
We are not in need

To be told
I love you
Before we fall asleep

The definition of insanity is...

The problem with I love yous
Is that
instead of that deep
Warm healing
Those words should bring

They are replaced
With fists and
tearful Apologies
With lies and credit swipes

Words used as a leash

The problem with I love you is
There is no love
Like that of

A Black woman

It heals and changes you
It holds and destroys you
It will be what saves us all

The problem with I love yous
Is that they are often
The first said
By the ones who
Know nothing of it

Who use it to abuse
And manipulate
To confuse and pontificate

The problems with I love yous
Is that those creatures and beings
Whom cannot speak
Show it in its purest forms
Abundantly

But we refuse to hear them
We refuse to see
With our logical ideas of love
We seem destined to keep

The problem with I love yous
Is the expectation that they come
With such high demands

a 20 carat ring

Financial security...

That they are harbingers
Of chaos and control
Unfettered jealousy
The problem with I love yous
Is how human words
Could never fully express

How we can't seem to
Get the timing right
How we wait to exchange them
Until we're under duress

Or how we capture them late
At night
In between rhythms and rocking

A drunken confession
Whispered on sweaty beds

The problem with I love yous
Is That they may never
Be said

How you thought of saying it
So many times in your head
Before you got that phone call
That Filled you with dread

The problem with I love yous
Is that we tried to capture God in words

Write the stars in our blood soaked
Alphabets

A non consensual contract
Forged by soulless white men

Finally their lies
Are Coming to a head

And so

As We recite the clunky syllables
From our dry colonized mouths

We lay with our mama Earth
To familiarize ourselves
Again

To see what love is all about

We dance and sing
and write and cry
Our new I Love Yous out

We work to speak the original language
Of our hearts
Trying to use what we can
To get back to the start

So as we say I love you
As we put the contract to bed
Let's reconnect to its essence

Let's build new worlds instead

-jade, sunrise 10/6/2020

OCEAN

My back is broad like the open desert
A sprawling and magnificent landscape
My legs strong and grounded like trunks of the trees you
played on
As a child...
My rough hands carry and lift you -

Never been too scared of hard work
Never been to scared to bleed

My body has grown, shafted and shifted.
Like I have. So many times.

We are learning the difference between each other.
When my mind takes over and leaves my sweet body
wanting.
Aching.
Shaking with the need to be seen
To be affirmed
To be released.
I glide my long fingers along this soft brown skin
This solar energy manifested
So hot
I squeeze and push deep on my muscles
On my tight spots.

My sweat drips down to meet the other wetness of me and
they swirl together until I disappear

Deep down into the ocean of myself

SHOWN LOVE

The ways I want to show and be shown love

I want love to spill out of my mouth
I want love to beat out of my chest

So loud
It wakes ya
Out Cha sleep

I want ta glideee
Through love
As I move
This great loving body
Cutting through energy air and pain.

I want love to blast through my fingertips
With a touch that'll set ya skin aflame
A snap of electrical currency

I want to have love as a wool blanket
That I can cover up in
To hide from the monsters
To protect me from the harsh elements of this life.

I want love to vibrate from the
Balance of my step

To the clap of my thighs
A blinking of eyes

Love love love
To hold me
To move me
And to soothe me

A love so pure
You can feel it in my anger
In my joy and in my pleasure

A love so good it'll
Change ya foreva

SACRED INHERITANCE

I inherited the pain of my mothers

The weight of this existence
The tired blood soaked hands

I feel the lash on my back
That crushing blow

I feel The sweat of our captors
dripping down my face

I inherited the loss of my mothers
The goodbye that never was

The rip
The tear
The distance
The snatching away

I am my mothers
And they are me
And we cut and clear and fight
With our machetes
We sift
And toil
We labor and love
Like none other

All of our lives

In this society
Who only seems
To want to eat us whole
These people who don't know if they want to
Be us
Fuck us
Or
Kill us

And still
We love we love we love

We clean the debris
We wash down the windows
We hold up the weight

I've been speaking with the Moon
And they tell me of all the things I was
Of all the things I am

I've been sitting with the Sun
And they tell me of all the light I hold
Of all the lives I've lived

Of all this sacred fire within
That I've *Inherited*

I've been sweeping my house up daily
Ridding myself of the trash and dirt
Others have tracked in

I've been speaking with my mothers lately

And they all tell me....

TREMENDOUS THING

I've always been a tremendous thing...

I see shadows of myself
Cast over skylines

As I walk
My footsteps tremble and shake
This earth

My laugh pulls tides
I fill rivers with my cries

When I dance
The earth tilts back and forth
on its axis

I change seasons

I know I'm here
For a mighty good reason

I've always been such a tremendous thing
Sometimes I'll break what's already fragile
Sometimes I leave craters
You may find yourself losing track
You may not find your way back

My gravity you may not grasp

I caress the canopies
Of trees
I splash my feet in the Pacific

I've always been such a tremendous thing

AND MY HEART SEIZES

With the unbearable grief of knowing
my lungs breath in deep
this filthy air

Of poison
Of dust, debris,
the ashes of our humanity

As my blood runs
blue
Black

As my feet tire of the
constant running

My knees ache from
This crouching position
Of
 helpless terror
Of terrible complicity

I let the crumble devastate me
And I stand
To bear the weight of witness
Of this great Death

I let my heart
Swell and
Beat and beat
I let my lungs breathe and breathe and breathe
I rest my tired feet and dress my wounds
I nourish in Spirit
Then I stand
And I fight.

MAKING A PROMISE OF MYSELF

A promise to myself
Making a promise out of these moments
Which come and go
With such a
Ferociousness

I'm done with
Kneeling at the gods of shiny things

I am done ripping myself open
In half's and half's and
I'm Halving again...

In quarters and in fifths
Into such teeny tiny things

My body felt so strange
in Wholes again

I tied a piece of bamboo on my finger
And wore it all day

And It felt like A promise

I'm not sure where it ended up

But I can't forget
 the tightness on my finger
That wet delicate
 fibrous strength

I can recall the meaning
I created out of folds and knots

And I remember the promises
I make
To myself

I'll make a million knots
to replicate and overwhelm
The promises
Made for me

I always seem to forget
How easy it can be
To unclench a fist
And I'll do it
Over and over

And over again ...